Quiet Thoughts

Short Poems
By Christopher Richmond

Christopher Richmond
15d Tetbury Street
Minchinhampton
Stroud GL6 9JG
Mobile: 07564 226821
Home: 01453 731192
Email: nailsworthchris@gmail.com

With Poems by Robert Law

First published 2022

Copyright © Christopher Richmond 2022

The right of Christopher Richmond to be identified as the author of this work has been asserted in accordance with the Copyright, Designs & Patents Act 1988.

All rights reserved. No part of this book may be reproduced, stored in a retrieval system, or transmitted in any form or by any means, electronic, electrostatic, magnetic tape, mechanical, photocopying, recording or otherwise, without the written permission of the copyright holder.

Published under licence by Brown Dog Books and
The Self-Publishing Partnership Ltd, 10b Greenway Farm, Bath Rd, Wick, nr. Bath BS30 5RL

www.selfpublishingpartnership.co.uk

ISBN paperback: 978-1-83952-507-0

Cover design by Kevin Rylands

Printed and bound in the UK

This book is printed on FSC certified paper

Quiet Thoughts

1962–2022

By Christopher Richmond

Contents

As You Love Us 6

All Alone *7*
All Change *7*
All Our Troubles *8*
All That's Left *8*
All There Is *8*
Already Over *9*
Ambition *9*
Apples *10*
As Darkness Falls *10*
As I Awaken *11*
As I Move Away *11*
Asleep To Dream *12*
As She Escaped *12*
At Sea *13*
Automaton *13*
Back To The Garden *13*
Beat Goes On, The *14*
Beating Of The Drum, The *14*
Benjamin Gunn *15*
Bit Of A Bore, A *15*
Boscombe Down *16*
Carisbrooke *16*
Cherry Tree *17*
Christmas Away *17*
Cold Wind, A *18*
Cover You Over *18*
Cricket *18*
Dance Dance Dance! *19*
Day After, The *19*
Dilys Meets Harry *20*
Don't Wait *20*
Door Opens, The *21*
Dustmen, The *21*
Earl's Court *22*
Easy Come *22*
Endless Street *23*
End Of The Line *23*
Epsom Downs *24*
Farewell *24*
First Day Of Spring *25*
Footsteps Follow *25*

Fragments *26*
Gone Forever *27*
Helicopter Flew Over, A *27*
Hope *28*
I Am What I Am *28*
I Board A Train *28*
I Called *29*
I Get Torn *29*
I Know A Place *30*
I Love You *30*
Impermanence *31*
In A Blink *31*
In A Jam *31*
In Perpetuity *32*
In Pieces *33*
In The Darkness *33*
Into The Deep *34*
I Remember *35*
It Really Doesn't Matter *35*
I've Wanted You *36*
I Woke Up *36*
I Would Do Anything *36*
Jolly Good Time, A *37*
Journey, The *37*
Koala *38*
Last Days, The *38*
Last Night *38*
Last Things *39*
Late Afternoon *39*
Leaving *40*
Leaving Home *40*
Let's Go *41*
Let The Wheels Roll *41*
Letting Go *42*
Life *42*
Life And Times *42*
Like A River Flow *43*
Little Children *43*
Little Light Relief, A *44*
Living In The Past *44*
Longing *44*
Long Time Ago, A *45*
Look At The River *45*

Lost 46
Loved And Lost 46
Love I Used To Know, A 47
Loving You 47
Make Way 48
Marchers, The 48
May Day 49
Midnight Struck 49
Mist On The Hills 50
More More More 50
Music 51
My Turn 51
Never Reaching The End 51
Never Too Late 52
Never To Return 52
Nobody Knows 52
No Going Back 52
No Longer Apart 53
No More 53
No Time To Stop 54
No Turning Back 54
No Use Holding On 54
Nowhere to Go 55
One Day 55
Only A Dream 55
On The Run 56
On Your Own 56
Open Arms 56
Otherworldliness 57
Our Last Time 57
Our Life 58
Out Of Mind 58
Out Of Nowhere 59
Parting, The 59
Party's Over, The 60
Passed Over 60
Paths Crossing 61
Ploughman I Will Be, A 61
Pray For Peace 62
Quickly Quickly 62
Quiet Moments 63
Remember 63
Return To East Coker 64
Sailed Out To Sea 64
Say 'Hi' To The Tillerman 65

Shadows 65
Silence 66
Silent Pools 66
Snow Came Early 67
Snowdrops 67
Someone Was Waiting 68
Something Stopped Him 69
So Silently 70
Speakeasy 70
Spring Is Here 71
Stan 71
Starting Over 72
Still Here 72
Still Time 73
Stranger 73
Suddenly 74
Sunset 74
Till Tomorrow 75
Time 75
Underground 76
Waiting 76
Walked 77
Walked Tall 77
What's To Do 77
When 78
When It Was Over 78
Why Should I Care? 78
Wind And Rain 79
Winter Into Spring 79

By Robert Law

Battle Of Messines 82
Engagement To 'Dolly' 84
Oh For A Smile Dear Love From Thee 86
The Night Has Overwhelmed The Day 87
Ever Children In Our Hearts
And Minds 88

As You Love Us

This poem is taken from Christopher Richmond's first book *Love Is The Way,* which contains 160 short contemplative poems written from a personal Christian perspective.

*As You
Love us
May we
Love You*

With all
Heart and
Soul
Mind and
Strength

Love our
Neighbours
As ourselves
Love our
Enemies

*In all
We feel
We think
We act
We are*

Love one
Another
Love You
Above
All other

All Alone

All alone
He walks
Alone

So far
Away from
Home

*Looking for
Something*

All alone
In her
Empty room

No one
Listens
No one
Cares

*All alone
Turned to
Stone*

All Change

*You go back
And everybody's
Moved on*

People and
Places change
Go out of
Range

Still a house
Upon the hill
And nothing's
Really
Changed

*Except you
Except me*

All Our Troubles

*All our
Troubles
Come from
Ourselves*

We try
To justify
Our words
And actions

Feel
Threatened
And want
To hit back

*We cannot
Ignore the
Consequences*

All That's Left

All I can see
Is your face
All over
The place

*Just to see
You smile
Makes it
All worthwhile*

All that's left
Is me and you
Loving you
The way
That I do

All There Is

Yesterday
Has gone
Tomorrow
Never comes

*Today is
All there is*

Look back
In vain
You have
Nothing
To gain

*The future
Takes care of
The past*

Live each
Moment
As if it's
Your last

Already Over

It's a
Long road
I've been
Travelling

*And I'm
Nearing
The end*

What's done
Is done
Cannot be
Undone

*It's all there
Waiting to
Happen*

It's
Already over
And it's
Hardly begun

Ambition

*Ambition's
Got the better
Of me*

Won't let me
Rest
Won't let me
Sleep

*Fear of
Slowing down
Being
Overtaken*

I am here
And want
To be there
I'm not happy
Where I am

*Ambition
That can
Only end in
Disappointment*

There is
No race
To be run
There is
No battle
To be won

*There are
No winners
There are
No losers*

Apples

Apples in
The orchard

Ladders
Leaning
Upwards
To the sky

Storing
Apples for
Winter

Watching
Boys
Turn into
Men

Old men
Die

They were
Getting old
And so
Was I

As Darkness Falls

As darkness
Falls
The darkest
Day

Stagnant
Pools
Silent still

Asleep
To dream
To rest
Awhile

This year
Into the next
New life
Out of old

The long
Awaited day
The afterglow

Time gone by
Where ghosts
Hang on

We pause
Still silent

See what
Spring will
Bring

We shall
Sing!

As I Awaken

Idly mocking
Those who
Mourn
He calls out
Along the shore

Fearsome
Mermen
Armed with
Stakes
Shake hands
With the
Faerie Queene

As I awaken
From a dream
Unchain
The captive
Slaves

As I Move Away

*I'm in the sky
And can't
Go back*

But always
Will remember
Those faces

*Those friends
Who came to
Say goodbye*

They'd given
So much
Expected
So little

*We may not
Meet again*

Their land
Disappears
Beneath
The clouds

*They stand still
As I move
Away*

Asleep To Dream

After lunch
We dozed off

Sunday
Afternoon
Resting
Ready for
Another week

Asleep
To dream
Float
Downstream

Woke up
For tea
At four o'clock

As She Escaped

As daylight
Followed night
Took flight

As I entered
The room
All went quiet

Caroline
Left by
The back door

Johnnie lay
Stretched out
Across
The floor

A rose branch
Scraped
Against the
Window pane

As she
Escaped
Into the rain

At Sea

Neptune
Lying dormant
Sleeping
On the sand

The captain
Welcomed us
Aboard
Said 'There's
Room for
Many more'

The cabin was
Deep down
And tight
The engines
Kept us awake
All night

Through
Darkness
We sailed
Hoping we
Would see
Light again

Looking
Shoreward
Forward
To another
Day

Automaton

It's the end of
The working
Week
And I'm
Getting paid

My boss's got
My number
And he's
Turning me
Into some
Kinda
Machine

Forgets
That I have
Feelings
Forgets
That I have
A soul

Back To The Garden

Back
To the garden

She sits
Up all night
In her
Nursery robe

Counting
The days
Looking for
Ways

Solitary
Seclusion

The Beat Goes On

*The beat
Goes on
Regardless of
Interruption*

The day
The world
Stopped
We stayed
Indoors

*Did not
Venture out*

We had
Overtaken
Nature
Or had nature
Overtaken us?

Turned our
Whole world
Upside down

*Turned it
Around*

Life would
Never be
The same

*We used
To be
So free*

The Beating Of The Drum

Taking down
The stalls
Sweeping up
The papers

*Counting
The takings
The makings
Of another day*

Take things
As they come
Listen to
The beating
Of the drum

*Take away
The structure
And what's
Left?*

Benjamin Gunn

Benjamin
Gunn
Thinks
He's the
Only one

*What have
You done
Benjamin
Gunn?*

Inspires us
With his
Emptiness

*His lack of
Self-control*

A Bit Of A Bore

I used
To think
You were
Funny

*You used
To make me
Laugh*

You're not
Funny
Anymore

*You're
A bit of
A bore*

I've heard
It all
Before

Boscombe Down

Fighter planes
Going up
And going
Down

*On Boscombe
Down*

Everybody
Holds hands
Makes a circle
Round
The town

*Flags line
The streets
The crowds
Cheer*

Carisbrooke

The
Carisbrooke
Donkey
Treads
The eternal
Wheel

*Brings
Water and
Wellbeing*

Round
And around
He goes
Look how
He goes!

*Turning
And returning*

Round
And around
On the
Merry-go-round

Cherry Tree

The
Cherry tree
Blossoms
And bears
Fruit

*Year after
Year*

Seasons
Come and
Seasons go

People
Come and
People go

*Renewal
And rebirth*

Christmas Away

And after work
We met at
Waterloo
Ready packed
To board the
Bournemouth
Belle

There was
A Christmas tree
For railway
Orphans
Ten thousand
Londoners
Were out to
Get away

Mainly young
Ones
Returning home
For Christmas
Is a family
Occasion
When no one
Should be
Alone

And as
I boarded
The train
The cold
Brought back
Memories

Of summer days
On the
Gold Coast
Of desolate
Sands
And surfing
Boards

A family
Reunion
Without their
Daughter
That distance
Could not
Separate

A Cold Wind

They're
Laying
Wreaths
At the
Cenotaph

*We were
On our way*

It was
A cold wind
That blew
Through
Épernay

Cover You Over

I'd cover you
With flowers
To pass
Away
The hours

Walk through
Showers
To watch
The moon
And stars

Cricket

A changing
Scene
Of cricket
On the
Village green

*White flannels
Wickets
And a ball*

The spectators
Clap
And soon
It's time for tea

Over and out
Long shadows
At the close
Of play

*White mist
Upon the green*

Phantom trees
Complete
The scene

Dance Dance Dance!

You only
Get out
What you
Put in

It's win
Win win!

You may
Not live
To see
Another day

So make
Hay
Live for
Today

You only
Get one
Chance

So dance
Dance
Dance!

The Day After

The day after
The day after
I think of you

Remember
All the happy
Times
We spent

One spirit
Lifting us up
Taking us
To another
Place

Discarded
Notes
Pictures
Of you

I called
But you
Did not
Answer

Where
Were you?

Dilys Meets Harry

*Dilys comes
Out of
The bingo
Hall*

Harry pokes
His head
Around the
Corner

*'They're in
The other bar'*

What makes
You think
You're so
Immortal?

Don't Wait

*Don't wait
It might be
Too late*

Don't let
Fear get
In the way
Don't let it
Be too long

Don't think
Too much
Don't do
Anything
Too much

Don't worry
About
Tomorrow
Tomorrow
Never comes

Don't cling
Get tied
To string
Have that
Final fling!

*Tomorrow is
Another day
We shall
Surely
Find a way*

The Door Opens

Jamie
Took me in

Said 'Billy
Where you
Been a
All night?

I been
Looking
For you
Everywhere'

There's
A knock
At the door
No one there

The telephone
Rings
Should I
Answer?

A key turns
In the lock
The door
Opens

The Dustmen

The dustmen
Told me of
Their journey

Whilst they
Were here

There were
Two world wars
And many
Died of hunger

Earl's Court

*A bedsit in
Earl's Court
All night
Parties*

*Get out of
Your seat
And onto
The street*

*Listen to
The beat
The sound of
Marching feet*

*I can
Take you
Higher
Walk along
The wire*

*Fill you with
Desire
Set your
Heart on fire*

Easy Come

Love
Comes
And goes

*Ebbs and
Flows*

Moves
So fast
Moves
So slow

*Easy come
Easy go
Love you
So*

Endless Street

I came in
From the
Cold
Lay in wait
An endless
Wait

With life
On hold
An endless
Night
No end
In sight

The smell
Of death
Was
Everywhere
Endless
Goings on

*I needed
To be
Heard*

Endless
Space
Endless
Time

*On endless
Street*

End Of The Line

The engine
Slowed
Down

*Ground to
A halt*

The end
Of the line
The end
Of time

Epsom Downs

Londoners
Pour out of
The station
And it's
Starting to rain

*View the city
From afar*

The ramblers
Saunter
The children
Gallop

*The sun
Comes out
And the roads
Steam*

The litter
Baskets
Are full
The iceman
Packs up

*There's
A storm brewing
And I can
Fly my kite*

Farewell

Farewell to
Ashtead village
And around
We hope we did
What we'd been
Planted for

Shading
And sheltering
Through all
Weathers
Acting as
Focal points
For all to see

But in all
Our years
Through war
And peace
We have found
Only vandals
Cut down trees

First Day Of Spring

*Down come
The goalposts
Up go the
Stumps*

An oily cap
A shovel
And a bucket
A plumber's
Bag of tools

*The sun's out
Let's go
For a picnic!*

Racehorses
Galloping
On the heath
Milk churns
Awaiting
Collection

Open-top
Buses
A matchstick
Pier
Deckchairs
Blown out
To sea

Draw the
Curtains
Empty the
Ashtrays

*First day
Of spring!*

Footsteps Follow

What feet
Have trod
This earthly
Sod?

*Footsteps
Follow to
The hollow*

Where
Britannia
Ruled
The waves

*Where
We lived
In caves*

Fragments

Cohesion
Then
Disintegration

In a
Fragmented
World
Without
A centre

Nothing holds

There are
No absolutes
Only a series
Of comings
And goings

Pieces of
The whole
Destined for
Oblivion

You grasp it
And it goes
It's gone
Before you
Know it

You cannot
Hold on

Hold on
And eventually
You have
To let go

We're all
Alone
Worlds within
Worlds

Locked in

Gone Forever

The sun
Comes up
The sun
Goes down

In deepest
Sorrow
I reach out
To you

Sadness
That sense
Of loss

Gone
Forever
Or was
It ever?

A Helicopter Flew Over

A helicopter
Flew over

Filled the
Garden
With white
Smoke

Then it all
Went dark

There were
Blinding
Flashes
In the sky
Intolerable
Heat

I felt myself
Slowly
Burning

With a prod
And a poke
All went up
In a puff
Of smoke

Hope

Hope
On the
Horizon

*Beckons
Me to call*

*Hoping
That you'd
Come
Through
Be true*

*Hope
Overcoming
Fear*

Wishing
You were
Here

I Am What I Am

*Part red
Part blue
Part Gentile
Part Jew*

I am
What I am
Just an
Average
Man

*Trying
To do
The best
He can*

I Board A Train

*I board
A train*

Knowing
Someone
Will be
Waiting
For me

*At the end
Of the line*

I can
No longer
Endure this
Loneliness

*I can
Hardly wait*

To be back
In your
Loving
Arms

I Called

I called
But you
Did not
Answer

*Where were
You?*

Were you
With
Somebody
New?

A love
That I
Never
Knew

*That wasn't
True*

We
Could not
Make it
Through

I Get Torn

*I get torn
Between
This and that*

Feeding
The cat
Wearing
A hat

*Things that
Remind me
Of you*

Between
Being born
And what
Comes next

*Between
This world
And the next*

Life as
We know it
And life
Beyond

I Know A Place

I know
A place
Where we
Can go

Where
Gentle
Waters
Flow

Above the
Cliffs at
Martinhoe

I Love You

*I love you
With all
My heart*

Don't ever
Want to be
Apart

*Let your
Feelings flow
And go go go!*

I love you
More than
You will
Ever know

*As you
Fade away
From view*

I love you
Just
The same

Impermanence

That moment
Lost forever

Impermanence
Haunts me so
Not knowing
Where I am

I like to feel
My feet
Upon the
Ground

I like to know
Where I am

A life
I thought
Would last
Forever

But nothing
Ever does

In A Blink

Time is
Shorter
Than you
Might think

In a blink

So quick
You have
No time
To think

In A Jam

Won't
Somebody
Tell me
What's
Going on?

I'm in
A jam
I don't
Know
Where
I am

In Perpetuity

In silence
Sleeps
The sultry day

*Omniscient
As it comes*

Saturation
Subsides
In sultry
Summer haze

*Swallow
Squadrons
Squawk*

In summer
There is
Winter
And autumn
There is
Spring

*Perpetual
Cyclical
Commensurate*

Perpetual
Rhythm
Perpetual
Haze
In rhythm
There is life

*In perpetuity
I cry*

Dilettante
Esmeralda
Dreams
Her life away

In Pieces

When
It all fell
Through
I wondered
What I'd do

*I felt so blue
I just didn't
Have a clue*

When you
Walked out
That door

Said you
Didn't
Love me
Anymore

*I took myself
Apart*

Picked up
The pieces
Made
A new start

In The Darkness

*In the
Darkness
Of the night*

They're not
There
When you
Want them

They put up
Barriers
You can't
Get through
To them

*I'm back on
That bridge
That derelict
Ship*

To reach
That certain
Point
To go
No further

*We're
Not alone*

We must
Listen
Try to
Understand

Into The Deep

We crossed
The desert
As night fell

The cartwheels
Turned
As the world
Turned

Entered
A walled town
Where the people
Wore black

Climbed
The mountain
Watched the river
Twist and turn

Ponies
Lapping at
The water's edge

The sun
Beat down
Waves crashed
Against
The rocks

There they were
Huddled
Together

Worn out men
With withered
Faces
Looking out
To sea

Mounted
The ponies
Rode into
The deep

I Remember

I remember
It well
What they
Tried to sell

The ringing
Of the bell
The picture
Of Little Nell

It was early
November
When we
Got back

And by
December
They had us
Making
Clay pigeons

It Really Doesn't Matter

It really
Doesn't matter
Who you are

*If you're rich
Or drive a car*

It really
Doesn't matter
What clothes
You wear

*The colour of
Your hair*

It really
Doesn't matter
What comes
Next

*It really
Doesn't matter
At all*

I've Wanted You

I've wanted you
For such
A long time

I've been
Going up
I've been
Going down

I've been
Going round
And round

Coming
And going
Not knowing
Which way
To turn

I've been
Doing this
I've been
Doing that

I've sailed
Across
Every sea

I've wanted you
For such
A long time

I Woke Up

I woke up
And they were
Still talking

I woke up
And they were
Walking away

I woke up
And you
Weren't there

Where were
You?

I Would Do Anything

I wish
There was
Something
I could do

To hold on
To this day

I would do
Anything
To be back
In that room

I wouldn't
Blame you
For leaving me

For going
On your way

A Jolly Good Time

*Didn't we have
A jolly
Good time?*

Had a laugh
Had a cry
Nothing by half
Never say die

Heads up high
When others
Were low

*Didn't we have
A jolly
Good time?*

The Journey

We drove
Through
The night

*Stopped off
At an
All night café*

Arrived in
The morning
Light

By the time
We got
There

*It was time
To come
Home*

It was
Too late

Koala

I wish
I was
A koala

Eating
Eucalyptus
Clinging to
A tree

Dreaming
My life
Away

The Last Days

The long
Summer days
The holidays

The last days
The parting
Of the ways

The late
Night film
Then the
Epilogue

The lights
Going out

Last Night

Last night
I saw your face

So real
I thought
You were there

You were
Happy
And so free

Just the way
You used
To be

Last night
I heard
Your voice

So clear
I thought
You were there

You sang
So softly

You were free
As free
As free can be

Your children
By your side

You didn't
Have to hide

Last Things

*The empty
Chair at the
Breakfast
Table*

*Sitting in the
Same room
Listening to
The same
Records*

*The doorbell
Rings
We talk of
Many things*

*If thoughts
Have wings
See what
The future
Brings*

Last things

Late Afternoon

*Late afternoon
In an
English tea
Garden*

*Fluffy
Scones with
Raspberry jam
And clotted
Cream*

*Lashings of
Earl Grey*

*They'll soon
Be clearing up
We haven't got
Far to go*

Leaving

*I look out of
My window
And what
Do I see?*

See you
Leaving
Suitcase
In your hand

*Without
A whisper
Without
A cry*

Leaving
Without
Saying
Goodbye

*Without
Saying why*

Leaving Home

*I looked out
Of the carriage
Window*

The whistle
Blew
The wheels
Began to turn

*They stood
On the platform
Waving me
Goodbye*

There was an
Eerie darkness
Like an eclipse

*Then hands
And faces
Faded*

I was alone
A young man
Left home
For the first time

Let's Go

Let's go
Inside
It's getting
Cold

*Let's have
Time away*

Pretend
Tomorrow
Is today

Let The Wheels Roll

*Come out of
Your houses
Spring is here!*

The cubs
Are back
From the
Church parade

Marching
In time
Carrying
Primroses

*No use
Dredging
The lake*

The air's
Electric
Reaches
Flashpoint

Don't touch
Metal
Keep away
From trees

Don't sneeze

Bill's beard's
Curling up
It's going
To rain

*Clouds
Closing in
Ambulances
Flash by*

Scatter
My ashes
Over the
Ganges

*Let the
Wheels roll*

Letting Go

Leaves
Letting go

Round
And around
They go

Not a sound

Falling to
The ground

Life

Life is
But short
And time
Can't be
Bought

Easier to
Take apart
Harder to
Put back

Life is
For living
Don't let it
Pass you by

Live life
To the full
And pull
Pull pull!

Life And Times

There are
Many ways
Of looking
At life

There will
Be times
When nothing
Rhymes

There's
No escape

There will
Come a time
When all
We have now

Will be
No longer

Like A River Flow

Like
A river flow
That you
Come and go

Like
The night
Watchman
I wake up
As others
Go to sleep

Like
Meteors
Floating
Aimlessly
Through space

We have
No base
No sense
Of place

Little Children

A small boy
In the river
Casting out

Children's voices
Echo in
The tunnel
The bell rings
And they return
To their classes

The chocolate man
From Kathmandu
Saves up all year
To give sweets
To little children

I've watched
My children grow
I've done
All of those things

If I were you
I wouldn't
Change a thing
I would hear
The children sing

A Little Light Relief

We all need
A little
Light relief

Belief in
Things
To come

Someone
To care
To share

Missing you
So much

Longing for
Your gentle
Touch

Living In The Past

Going round
In circles
Getting
Nowhere
Fast

I knew
It wouldn't
Last
I was living
In the past

Longing

You say
You don't
Want my love

You want
The stars
Above

Longing for
Something

That isn't
There

You look
Forward
To that day

Then it's
Taken away

A Long Time Ago

I think
I've been
Here before

*A long long
Time ago*

I squirm
Knee-deep
In mud

*And open up
The coalhouse
Door*

Look At The River

*Look at
The river*

See how
She slips
And slides

*How silently
She glides*

Guides me
To another
Place

*Slowly
Gathers
Pace*

Rides and
A lot more
Besides

Lost

He looked
At her
And she
Looked
At him

*Then looked
The other
Way*

He's lonely
And he's
Sad

*He's lost
The only girl
He ever
Had*

He never
Lived
A normal
Life

*And all
He longed for
Was a wife*

Loved And Lost

*To get
So far*

And then
Be told
You can go
No further

*You have
To turn
Around*

Better
To have
Loved
And lost

*Never mind
The cost*

A Love I Used To Know

*The snow
Is falling
And I hear
You calling*

*A love
I used
To know*

*That isn't
Here
Anymore*

*A love
I used
To know*

*That melted
In the snow*

*A world
We used
To share*

*That isn't
Here
Anymore*

Loving You

*Love can
Break
Your heart
In two*

*Feel
Your heart
Flutter
Hurry home
For supper!*

*Loving you
Loving me*

*It's not
Easy
But we
Can try*

Make Way

I open
My eyes
As a nurse
Wheels in
A trolley

One life
Ends as
Another
Begins

The setting
Of the sun
When this
Earthly work
Is done

Make way
For the
Living!

The Marchers

Triumphant
Are the
Marchers
For they
Go on

Fighting
For freedom

Security won
For the
Immediate
Future

Struggle
Sometimes
Leading to
Loss of life

But never
A tear
Wasted

May Day

The war
Drum's
Beating!

The
Shopkeeper
Stands
At his door
Waiting for
Customers

He cries
'That's
Enough!'
But it's only
The beginning

Ours
Had been
A hard life

On May Day
We polish
Our guns
And sing
'The Red Flag'

Midnight Struck

Midnight struck
And with it
Came another
Year

Measured time
Is difficult
To endure

No backward go
Let it grow
Move forward
With the flow

It won't
Come again
The first time
Is the last

Once and
Once only

Mist On The Hills

*They were
Married in the
Morning light*

There was
Mist on the hills
And a church
In the valley

The parish
Priest
Shook hands
With his
Congregation

And the
Patients
Walked out of
The cottage
Hospital

More More More

*Much much
Much too much*

When enough
Is not enough
The going
Gets tough

*Striving
Never arriving
Still wanting
More*

Short-lived
Pleasures
Leaving us
Feeling empty

*The more
We have
The less
It's worth*

What's it all for
Wanting
More more more?

Music

Woke up
To birdsong

Shovelled
Sand
In the
Builders'
Yard

Listened to
To the
Band

Every night
I hear
Music

Takes me
Where
I want to go

My Turn

I looked
For you
Everywhere

Looked back
On happy
Days

The family
Had grown
Older

Moved on

And now
It was
My turn
To return

Never Reaching The End

The sailor's
Wife looks
Vacantly
Out to sea

As his yacht
Disappears
Over the
Horizon

He sails on
Never
Reaching
The end

Never Too Late

It's never
Too late
To change
Your mind

To open
Your heart
And make
A new start

Never To Return

The last of
The tourists
Gone home

*The hotels
All boarded up*

The house
Empty
The garden
Overgrown

*The owner left
Never to
Return*

Nobody Knows

*Nobody knows
Which way
The wind
Blows*

Where
The river
Flows
Where time
Goes

*If there's
Life out there*

We're coming
And going
All of the time

*Searching for
Something
We'll never
Find*

No Going Back

The door
Was open
So I entered

*The door
Closed*

I knew
There
Would be

*No going
Back*

No Longer Apart

Cut off
From each
Other
Shut off
From the
World

My heart
In silence
Stands
With you
Understands

Your hands
In mine
Entwine

Your warm
Embrace
Meeting
Face to
Face

Each to
Each
No need
Of speech

Come
Summer
Heat
And winter
Chill

It will pass

We shall
Meet again
All the
Stronger

No longer
Be apart

No More

No more
Greed and
No more
Need

No more
Wars and
No more
Cause

No more
Heartache
No more
Pain

No more
Gain

No Time To Stop

There's
No time to stop
On your way
To the top

*Stay ahead
Or get
Left behind*

Aim high
Don't be shy
Look it
In the eye

*Don't let it
Pass you by*

You can
Make it
If you try

No Turning Back

*We know
Our beginning
But not
Our end*

We move
Forward
And nothing
Can stop us

We lose track
There will be
No turning
Back

*We know
So much
But are we
Any wiser?*

No Use Holding On

No use
Holding on
Our love
Has been
And gone

*Something
To do
To stop
Feeling blue*

To every low
There is a high
A place to go
A reason why

Nowhere To Go

Lost in
The desert
With night
Closing in

Hungry and
Thirsty with
Nowhere
To go

One Day

One thing
Leads to
Another

*We keep
Ourselves
Busy*

One day
A year
The road
Was closed

*One year
The river
Froze*

Only A Dream

*I saw it
In a dream*

A girl
I used
To know
Lay
Motionless
Beside
A stream

It's not
What it
Seems
It's only
A dream

*Floating
Downstream*

On The Run

The stray dogs
On the
Waste-ground
Howl at night

There's
A storm raging
The boats
Have left
Their moorings

Tracker dogs
And roadblocks
On the moor
Two convicts
On the run

*One with
A gun*

On Your Own

I'm wondering
What you're
Doing

*Now you're
On your own*

I'm wondering
Where you're
Going

*Now you're
All alone*

Open Arms

The waters
Rose
And flooded
Our lands

*We held
Hands*

The children
Smiled
Through rags

*Invited us
Into their
Houses*

Welcomed us
With open
Arms

Otherworldliness

A universe
Interspersed
With planets
And with stars

Infinite

Other worlds
Such as ours
Counting
The hours

Eternal

They look
At us
We look
At them

Our Last Time

Our paths
Crossed
Many years
Ago

*I've forgotten
How it was*

We didn't
Know it
At the time
But it was
To be

*Our last time
Together*

Our Life

It was a
Backstreet
Room
In a Midland
Town

A little cold
At night
But a blanket
Kept us warm

There was
A table
And two chairs
And a picture
Above the stairs

We went to
Church
On Sunday
Went back
To work
On Monday

On Tuesday
They emptied
The bins and
On Friday
The laundry van
Passed by

Children played
Outside
Their parents
Stayed indoors

Seasons came
And seasons
Went
People came
And people went

It was a
Backstreet
Room
In a Midland
Town

A little cold
At night
But a blanket
Kept us warm

Out Of Mind

We distance
Ourselves

Afraid of
What we
Might find

What's
Left behind
Is intertwined

Out of mind

Out Of Nowhere

Out of ashes

Rising
Wilting

Out of
Nowhere

White horses
Carrying
Messengers

Movements
Becoming
Part of cycles

The Parting

It ended
Where it started
They parted

A full moon
The longest day
Walked down
To the river
Sat upon
The bridge

That whatever
Was between
Them
Was no longer
Maybe
Never was

Love offered
But not
Reciprocated
Meaning
Separation

He walked
Upstairs
Where once
They slept
And now
In different
Rooms

What meant
So much
Means
So little now
But he still
Loves her
And always will

One of the
Saddest days
The parting of
The ways

The Party's Over

Now
The party's
Over
We've
Had our
Fling

We don't
Need
To worry
About
A thing

*Like the
Runaway
Train
I was out of
Control*

Passed Over

*The clouds
Scattered*

And the rain
Spattered
On the
Old tin roof

*Drip drop
Drip drop
Pitter-patter
Pitter-patter*

The rain
Stopped
And we came
Out of
Our houses

*Passed over
In a shower
Of rain*

Paths Crossing

Passageways
Of people
Flowing
Periodically

Above
And below
They tread

Voices
Reminding me
There are
People

Paths crossing
Never to meet
Again

A Ploughman I Will Be

A ploughman
I will be

I'll furrow
Fields
I'll come
I'll go
I'll reap
I'll sow

I'll make
Things grow

Pray For Peace

Pray for
Peace

Amongst
People
Amongst
Nations

For war
To cease
To find
Release

For leaders
And the led
The living
And the
Dead

Peace
On earth
Goodwill
To all

To put
An end
To war
To fight
No more

Sword to
Plough

No one
Wins
We all lose

Quickly Quickly

You better
Take heed
It's speed
Speed
Speed

Moving
So fast
Each
Moment
Could be
Your last

Never
Stopping
To see

Quiet Moments

Go to places
Where we
Used to go

Meeting
Friends
We used to
Know

Quiet
Moments
Such as these

Your words
Whispering
In the breeze

Remember

Remember
How it used
To be

Two rounds
Of toast
And a pot
Of tea

Remember
The backroom
Boys

The men in
The engine
Room

Remember
The good times
Forget the bad

Be happy
Not sad

Return to East Coker

All is silent still
I must not stop
I must keep
Moving on

Through red rocks
I burrow
Sunken lanes
Leading me down
To East Coker
On a wet afternoon
In June

In the teashop
I shelter
From the rain

Enter a dark wood
Where no one goes
The lights go out
We must leave
In order to arrive

Who knows
What spring
Will bring?

Each moment
Is a new beginning
The yearning
The burning
The not knowing
Where we're going

The endless cycle
Of birth and rebirth

Darkness falls
Across the fields
Through pillars
And a wooded glade
To St Michael's
Church

Sailed Out To Sea

We mended
Our nets
And sailed
Into the night

By dawn
Our nets
Were full
So we turned
For home

Anchored up
And rowed
Ashore

Sailed
Out to sea
Got back
In time
For tea

Say 'Hi' To The Tillerman

A phantom
Ship
A calm sea

See the
Dredger
In the sea
Mist
Beach huts
Like sentry
Boxes

The year
The seawall
Collapsed
We sent
Blankets

Time passes
Slowly
On these long
Summer
Days

Rivers of
Light
Running
Down
The road

The clouds
Blow over
The sun
Shines
Through

Do what you
Believe in
Say 'Hi'
To the
Tillerman

Shadows

They come
They go
Like shadows
In the night

Shadows
Seen and
Unseen
What might
Have been

The
Unfamiliar
Becoming
Familiar

Then seeing
Everything
For the very
Last time

Silence

Snowflakes
Falling
To the ground

Not a sound

Silence in
The churchyard
Separating
Me from you

My heart aches

The deathwatch
Beetle
In the belfry
Tower

The church
Clock
Striking on
The hour

*Silence
Breaking us
Apart*

Broken glass
Keepsakes
Of a world
Intact
Lost contact

*My soul
Awakes*

Silent Pools

A new day
Breaks
The city
Awakes

The property
Tycoon
Surveys
The city
From his
Penthouse

She walks
Alone
In empty
City streets

The army
Deserter
Hides
Unaware
The war is
Over

We lived in
The valley
Till they
Flooded us out

Our children
Grow up
Leaving us
Behind

Silent pools
In dark forests

Waiting for
The sun
To shine

Snow Came Early

Snow came early
That year
Blanketing
The mountains

We skated
On the lake
Eyed icicles
On the
Fountains

Snow-covered
Hedges
Gushing rivers
Towering firs

Snow came early
That year
Blanketing
The mountains

Snowdrops

Back to
The river

Snowdrops
Cluster
On the bank
Where we
Used to sit

And watch
The river
Flow

Someone Was Waiting

Weary of carrying
His own cross
He even talked
To himself
He was that lonely

*I watched him
Barricade himself in
Then fight
To get out*

He sat in the corner
His face looked
So out of place
He had no friends
Nowhere to go

*No place
He could call his own
His home*

Like an alien
A stranger in
This life
No one listened
To him
And he pleaded
No pity

*There was
An impenetrable
Gulf*

Everybody else
Moved in twos
He was
The odd man out
Loneliness was
Of his own making
His best friend

*He had learnt
To live with himself*

That afternoon
He ascended
The hill
In an autumn mist

*Sat in silence
And watched
The sunbeams
Flicker*

Then returned to
An empty house
But he was
Not alone

*Someone was
Waiting*

Something Stopped Him

The dancers
Screamed with joy
And music
Flowed down
From the
Mountainside

He wanted
To reach out
But something
Stopped him

The man
In the corner
Looked so alone
So out of place
Something
Stopped him
From coming out

There were
Bright lights
And amplifiers
I wished he could
Lose himself
Lose control

They were
The instigators
They identified
With others
He identified
Only with himself

In a darkened
Room
They danced
To the rhythm

So Silently

He emptied
His heart
Replaced
His feelings
With theirs

So involved
With their lives
That he ignored
His own

His life
Seemed to go
A fleeting by
And however
Hard he tried
He could not
Seem to
Find his way

He seemed
To pass
Unnoticed
And no one
Missed him
When he went

So silently
He moved

Speakeasy

We touched
Down at
Cape Town

The wind
Blew through
The terminal
Building

Entered
A speakeasy
Bar

Outside
A world
Built around
The motorcar

Spring Is Here

Summer birds
Take flight

A gentle
Upland breeze
A buzz of
Bumblebees

Baby bats
Wake up to
Spring

Green shoots
In the woodland
New life
Out of old

A late
Goodnight

I'll meet you
In the
Early morning
Light

The sun
Breaks through
The sky
Turns blue

It's a new day
Spring is
Here

Awaken to
The chorus!

Stan

Out in
All weathers

Sporting his
Leathers
Preening his
Feathers

He's Stan
The all-
Weather
Man

Starting Over

I see
All my past
Go in front
Of me

*Our memories
Play tricks*

We may
Choose
To forget

*What's
Lost in
Remembering?*

I'm going back
Where I
Came from

*I'm going to
Start all over
Again*

Still Here

*I will live
In your
Future*

And you
Can live
In my
Past

*I will still
Be here*

When
Everybody
Else
Has been
And gone

Still Time

As water
Wears away
The rock
The tick-tock
Of the clock

An old man
Contemplates
His life
Spread out
Upon a table

Waves
Washed against
The seawall
And the world
Seemed eternal

Our lives
Almost over

There were
Things
We'd do
We'd never
Do again

But there was
Still time

Stranger

A stranger
Lives in
Danger

Has no
Roots

Only
The boots
He's
Standing in

Suddenly

Suddenly
It all went
Dark

About to rain

I saw you
In the distance
Walking back
To me

The rain
Came down
We went
Indoors

*Sat down
And talked*

I loved you
Like I never
Did before

A bird flew in

The rhythm
Taking us
To another
Place

Sunset

*Here I stand
On dry land
The offing
In full view*

The sun
Sinking on
The horizon
Silhouettes of
Fishermen
Returning

Sitting on
The verandah
Watching
The sun
Go down

*She knitting
He tending
His flowers*

The shadows
Lengthen
There's a chill
In the air

Till Tomorrow

I see your
Reflection
In the river

And hear
Your footsteps
Follow in
The distance

I see your face
It beckons me
To love you

Because
To know you
Is to love you
And accept you
The way
You are

I lay myself
Beside you
Till tomorrow

Time

Time
Slipped by
And we
Hung on

Time
And space
That knew
No bounds

Time
Separating
Me
From you

Time
Present
Now
Time past

Underground

Burrowing
Beneath
The city streets

*Dreaming of
Summer
Holidays*

No voices
Just mechanical
Sounds

*Doors open
Doors close*

It's the
Chelsea
Flower Show
And I'm
Thinking of

*Emigrating to
Australia*

Outside
Sunlight
Dazzles

*The clatter of
Pneumatic
Drills*

Waiting

*Waiting for
Something
That never
Comes*

Standing
At the station
Not reaching
My final
Destination

*Some day
When we're
Not so
Far away*

Steps
Leading
Down to
The sea

*A steamship
Waiting at
The quay*

Walked

Walked in
The long
Grass

*Paddled
In the
Tillingbourne*

Walked
Across
The salt marsh

*With a lantern
In my hand*

Walked Tall

He grew taller
And his world
Got smaller

*Walked tall
Above it all*

Came down
From the
Mountain

*Drank from
The fountain*

The closer
He got
The less
It made
Sense

What's To Do?

What's to do
In this
Empty town?

*Young ones
On street
Corners*

The picture
Houses
All closed
Down

When

When
The last cent
Is spent

*All the
Shouting
Over*

When
The words
Won't flow

*There's
Nowhere
To go*

When this
Restless
World

*Is silent
Still*

We shall
Return
To the
Garden

When It Was Over

I knew
When it
Happened

*I knew
You'd be
The one*

And when
It was over

*You and me
We'd had
Our fill*

I felt
So empty

*I felt
So alone*

Why Should I Care?

Cumin
And coriander
Arboreal
Salamander
Demetrius
And Lysander

*Why should
I care?*

Wind And Rain

I'm down
In the
Valley

*Rain
Running
Down*

*Up a blind
Alley*

*On the
Dark side
Of town*

Wind and rain
Wind and rain

*When shall
I see you
Again?*

Winter Into Spring

We slept
Most of
The winter
To escape
The cold

Woke up
To silence
On the
First day
Of snow

*All lay
Dormant
Ready for
Spring*

War And Love Poems

1914–1915

By Robert Law

Battle Of Messines

Poem by my grandfather, Private Robert Law of the 14th Battalion City of London (London Scottish). He was wounded at the Battle of Messines in October 1914.

I sing of the battle of the flood
Where our brave lads lay in the mud
And o'er beyond lay the German guns
Worked by stalwart boys called Huns

The night wore on and to sleep they tried
But just as their eyes became less wide
The order rang out through the air
'To Arms, the Germans they are there'

Now then Scottish give them the bayonet
O'er there's the trench and you must gain it
Scarce were the words spoken loud
The Scots are at them like a cloud

O'er yards and yards the rush was wild
And on to Germans deeply filed
West London's Corps of Scots so grand
And bent the Germans to the ground

Wild raged the fight on every side
But keener eyes ne'er steel did guide
Than those who wear the Hodden Grey
So soon our Scottish had its way

Again, again come German hosts
In which Bavarians number most
Again, again they're beaten back
For never force can beat our Mack

The fight is desperate 'Strike Sure'
Dear London Scots the day is yours
Fight, yes fight with all your might
For London, love and all that's right

Well they fight and with strong will
Yet the German hosts are before them still
More loudly grows the battle's clatter
Until at last the Germans scatter

Now above the battle's lessened din
Comes the shrieking of the wind
Bearing awful cries at night
Cries of men in desperate plight

Then horrible the morning broke
And showed what fell before their strike
Ah no! I'll say little of the blood
That lay upon the plains of mud

It is remembered to this day
How our manly lads in grey
With swinging kilts and hearts aglow
Rushed at Britain's greatest foe

How well each man bore the fight
And severed the proud German's might
All honour to the Hodden Grey
'Strike Sure' Scottish, yes that's the way

Dear Scottish were you on England's shore
With well earned peace for evermore
How each Londoner's heart to you would go
For that great and good and mealy blow

Oh Scottish let us hear once more
The gallant cry we've heard before
We too will sing with you that day
'Way! Way! for the Hodden Grey'

Engagement To 'Dolly'

*Engagement poem by my grandfather, Robert Law ('Bobby')
to my grandmother, Constance Pike ('Dolly') in February 1915.
After serving in the Battle of Loos in September 1915,
'Bobby' married 'Dolly' in November 1915.*

How many and many a time
Do thought and time combine
Each to each and all to all
Fond past memories to recall

Fondest of all past days
Marks the meeting of two ways
Two ways of life I mean to say
That met upon a certain day

The day is cherished o'er and o'er
And each year will see it cherished more
For thoughts of past happiness
Always keeps us truly blessed

Of all the days that make the year
Now doth the happy-est appear
For on this day my love did say
Come dear heart to me alway

I came to that heart so full of love
And thought I'd reached heaven above
And still I think that thought is right
For love to love is this world's might

As gentle as the dove my girl
Will this heart for ever thrill
And ever pray for me no harm
And God to keep my heart in charm

Oh love! of God it is a gift
To give unhappy souls a lift
To higher things and joyfulness
Especially when the soul's hard pressed

Then, oh Dolly! how can I say
All the happiness you gave that day
The day when first I clasped your breast
And held it tight against my chest

I can but thank and love you well
And always shall I love to tell
How good and noble and so true
A love I have; and also you

Keep, oh keep this heart of mine
Closely folded next to thine
Keep it where all pleasure grows
Fill it till it overflows

I love you more than I can say
And hate to be so far away
But some fair day for which I long
I'll be with you and sing a song

You will not find my song in book
But in my heart for it must look
And there you'll find what I sing
Flows from love's lovely spring

So once again I hail the return
Of the day on which your heart was won
For double doth the pleasure grow
And love for ever – it will glow

Further love I would you knew
How happy is a love that's true
And more; it's stronger than a tree
Fairer than the flowers we see

Oh when this day doth next appear
And adds to time another year
May our hearts remain aglow
With the love that was a year ago

And as the years go past at length
And take away our body's strength
May we snuggle closely to each other
And defy old time our love to smother

Oh For A Smile Dear Love From Thee

Oh for a smile dear love from thee
'Twould banish all my sorrow
And make my sleep unwakeful be
Dreaming until the morrow

Oh for one kiss (that's what I miss)
'Twould make me dwell in joy
And make it more and more my wish
To always be your boy

Oh for one fond embrace
To cheer this drooping heart
Oh that my chest your breast did grace
And never more to part

Oh for a life lived with thee
My fond dear sweetheart
I should then always happy be
And never from you part

And happier thoughts I send to thee
Who art my sweetheart ever
It is a wish that we should be
In future parted never

Oh for two lives to combine
Never more to part
And love to triumph over time
Resting heart to heart

The Night Has Overwhelmed The Day

The night has overwhelmed the day
The worker from the field
Should his broad ploughshare stay
From raising the grassy field

Now with no strong high lifting tread
The farmer regains his cot
For o'er his place is covered red
Of loved ones picked and shot

He gripped his ploughshare tight
Dark glared his eye of blue
He saw the advance of German might
And wondered what to do

'To do!' yes that's it loud he cried
As his loved fields they trampled o'er
And from the plough a bayonet raised
To defend his own beloved door

But Germany has many war hounds
Who tear at the peaceful throat
So brave Belgium is outside his bounds
But still he keeps his tot

This year our brave worker again will turn
His ploughshare over the soil
And he the German hosts will spurn
Having taken away their spoil

So roll on 1915 dearest year
And with the earliest ray
Of morning cast one fair tear
Of peace on earth alway

Ever Children In Our Hearts And Minds

Oh what a lovely sight to see
A child upon its bended knee
Lisping with its lips so neat
A prayer to God in accents sweet

There upon its little bed
Gently resting is its head
The innocent head with reverence bent
All the while the prayer is sent

Its prayer is from a mother's heart
Who fondly listens as the words depart
And hopes within her loving breast
Her child always will be blest

The child into a man will grow
And into this world will surely go
Yet at all times of trouble sad
Of these childhood days be glad

Yes lovely are the childhood days
Free from error and bad ways
Free from temptations strong and wild
Ever always soft and mild

The dear God in Heaven above
Keep us in thy bounteous love
Ever children in our hearts and minds
Ne'er regretting what's behind